KWANZAA FUN

LINDA ROBERTSON
ILLUSTRATED BY JULIA PEARSON

Kingfisher
NEW YORK

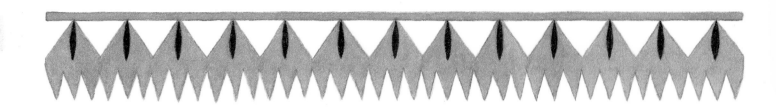

Kingfisher
Larousse Kingfisher Chambers Inc.
95 Madison Avenue
New York, New York 10016

First edition 1996
2 4 6 8 10 9 7 5 3 1

LIBRARY OF CONGRESS CATALOGUING-IN-PUBLICATION DATA
Robertson, Linda.
Kwanzaa fun / Linda Robertson, Julia Pearson.—1st ed.
p. cm
Summary: Presents activities and crafts to celebrate the seven
principles of the holiday which celebrates African American cultural
heritage.
1. Kwanzaa—Juvenile literature. 2. Afro-Americans—Social life
and customs—Juvenile literature. 1. Kwanzaa. 2. Kwanzaa
decorations. 3. Handicraft. 4. Pearson, Julia. II. Title.
GT4403.R63 1996
394.2'61—dc20
96-7809 CIP AC

Edited by Nancy Bliss

Printed in Spain

CONTENTS

The History of Kwanzaa

Kwanzaa is a holiday that celebrates the African tradition of gathering together at the end of the harvest. It was created in 1966 by Dr. Maulana Karenga, a professor and cultural leader. He wanted to help African Americans to remember their heritage. He also hoped Kwanzaa would be an annual reminder of the importance of sharing with family and friends, and that this would help build a sense of African-American community throughout the United States.

Kwanzaa begins on December 26 and lasts until January 1. There is a principle for each day of Kwanzaa. These seven principles help us to think about our lives and future, and promote a sense of pride in African-American culture.

The word kwanzaa comes from the African trade language Swahili. In Swahili, *kwanza* is a word from a phrase which means "first fruits." Dr. Karenga added an extra "a" to remind us that it is different from the original word.

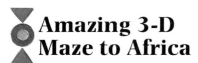

Amazing 3-D Maze to Africa

You will need
ball of yarn • tape • piece of paper • a small drawing of Africa • prize for the winner

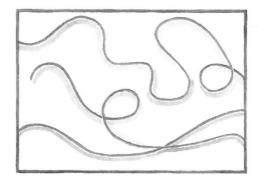

1. Cut a piece of yarn 4 or 5 feet long for each player. Tape one end of each piece of yarn to the piece of paper.

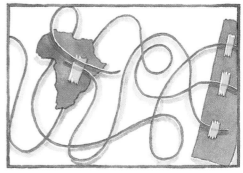

2. Out of sight of the players, have an adult attach the map of Africa to one end of one of the pieces of yarn.

The Seven Days of Kwanzaa

December 26
Unity

Umoja
(oo-MOE-jah)

December 27
Self Determination

Kujichagulia
(koo-jee-cha-goo-LEE-ah)

December 28
Collective Work & Responsibility

Ujima
(oo-JEE-mah)

Use the seven principles to improve yourself and to help others.

December 29
Cooperative Economics

Ujamaa
(oo-JAH-mah)

December 30
Purpose

Nia
(nee-AH)

December 31
Creativity

Kuumba
(koo-OOM-bah)

January 1
Faith

Imani
(ee-MAH-nee)

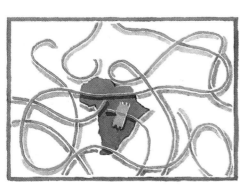

3. The adult should then mix up all of the yarn, creating a large, loose tangle—but not too tangled!

4. Remove each piece of yarn from the paper and give one end to each player. Untangle the maze to find who gets to Africa!

Kwanzaa symbols

To celebrate Kwanzaa with your family, put the seven symbols of Kwanzaa on a low table each night during the holiday. Kwanzaa symbols help teach and strengthen the basic principles of Kwanzaa. The kikombe (*kee-COAM-bay*) is the cup that symbolizes unity. It is used only in the libation ceremony (see page 10). Here are the other symbols of Kwanzaa.

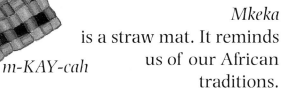

m-KAY-cah

Mkeka
is a straw mat. It reminds us of our African traditions.

Vibunzi
are ears of corn. They remind us of the importance of children.

vi-BUN-zee

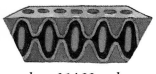

kee-NAH-rah

Kinara
is a seven-branch candle holder. It says that we all came from the same place.

Mazao
are the fruits and vegetables of the harvest. They remind us of the rewards of working together.

mah-ZAH-oh

sah-WAH-dee

mee-SHOO-maah sah-BAH

Mishumaa Saba
are the seven candles that remind us of the principles of Kwanzaa. We light one each day, beginning with the black one in the middle.

6 4 2 1 3 5 7

Zawadi
are the gifts. Handmade gifts are given at Kwanzaa for work well done and to encourage children to practice the seven principles all year long, not just during Kwanzaa.

Kinara and Mishuma Saba

You will need
red, green, and black construction paper (8½" x 11")
● scissors ● glue ● double-sided tape ● paint or glitter

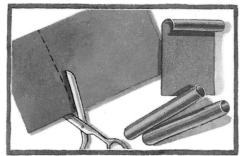

1. Fold one piece of the paper into thirds the long way. Decorate the outside. Place double-sided tape along the long edges of the paper on the inside only.

2. For candles, cut sheets of construction paper in half the short way. Roll three pieces each of red and green paper, and one of black, into tubes. Secure them with tape.

3. Stand the candle holder upright. Bring one end of the paper up and stick the candles in position. Bring the other end of the paper up and press the edges together.

4. To make the candle flames, cut out flame shapes and color them yellow or add glitter. Tape a flame to the inside of the black candle on the first day of Kwanzaa. "Light" the red candle next to it on the second day, then the green, and so on.

Special phrases

There are some important phrases used in the Kwanzaa celebration. These phrases are in the African language of Swahili. You can learn these basic Swahili words by sounding them out. You can practice speaking the Swahili words that are part of the Kwanzaa celebration with your family and friends.

Habari Gani (*ha-BAH-ree GAH-nee*)
During Kwanzaa we greet each other by saying "Habari Gani," which means "What's new?" Answer by saying the name of the principle being celebrated that day. On the first day of Kwanzaa when someone says "Habari Gani," you answer by saying "Umoja." On day five of Kwanzaa, when someone says "Habari Gani," your answer should be "Nia."

Harambee (*hah-ROM-beh*)
The harambee means "Let's pull together." It is the Kwanzaa call for unity. The harambee is performed in sets of seven to honor the seven principles. The harambee should be done after the libation ceremony and at the end of the celebration, but it can also be done on any occasion when you want to strengthen the spirit of unity.

Family Tree

You will need
1 yard of 45-inch wide muslin • glue • red and green fabric paint • paintbrush • black felt • stapler • wooden dowel • rope or yarn • newspaper

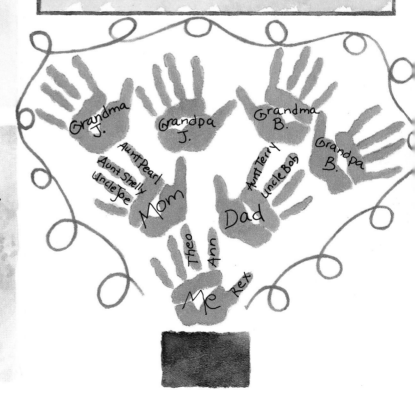

Welcome Banner

Fold each piece of felt in half the long way and cut into two pieces. Then fold each piece in half again (but do not cut!) to make ten folded pieces.

You will need
5 pieces of felt 8½ x 11 inches • at least 3 yards of 1-inch wide ribbon • scissors
• acrylic writing paint (or glitter and glue)
• double-sided tape or glue

Paint one letter of the word "HABARI GANI" on the front of each piece of felt and let dry. Spread the ribbon out and tape or glue each piece of felt to the ribbon in its fold. Make sure you space each letter equally.

1. Put down newspaper to protect your work surface. Cut a tree trunk shape slightly larger than your hand from the black felt. Glue securely at the center bottom of the muslin. Squirt red fabric paint on your hands and smooth it over your palms.

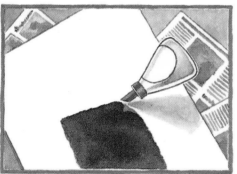

2. Carefully place your palm down above the middle of the top of the tree trunk. Above your handprint, make two prints for your parents. Finally, make four more on top for your grandparents. Then go back and write in all the names of your relatives.

3. Finish your family tree by painting a green loop of leaves around the handprints. To hang it up, fold the top of the muslin over two inches and staple closed, as shown. Slide in the dowel and tie yarn to each end. Display your heritage proudly!

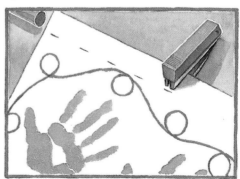

The Libation Ceremony

The Kwanzaa libation ceremony is very important. It begins with an older and respected friend or member of the family giving a toast. The toast is made to honor and praise our ancestors. Then the libation (water or juice) is sprinkled from the unity cup (a special cup that is only used for this purpose) onto the floor in the four directions: east, west, north, and south. The libation reminds us of the presence of the ancestors, and offering them a drink to quench their thirst keeps them alive in our memory. After giving the ancestors a drink, the unity cup is passed around and each member of the family takes a sip.

Libation Toasts

1. To our ancestors: let us honor and praise them and keep our memories of them alive
2. To the future
3. To children, our hope for the future
4. To building a strong community
5. To education, our children's key to the future

 ## Unity Cup

The cup used for the libation ceremony is called the unity cup, or kikombe (*kee-COAM-bay*) in Swahili. You can make your own cup for this special occasion.

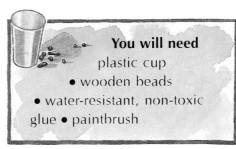

You will need
plastic cup
• wooden beads
• water-resistant, non-toxic glue • paintbrush

1. Brush a generous amount of glue around the outside of the cup. Leave about $\frac{3}{4}$ inch unglued around the rim. Let the glue dry until it is slightly tacky.

2. Press beads onto the cup to make a beautiful African design. Leave space around the rim so you can drink from it safely. Let it dry thoroughly.

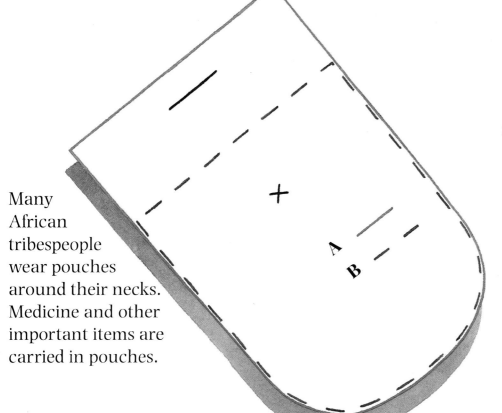

Many African tribespeople wear pouches around their necks. Medicine and other important items are carried in pouches.

You will need
felt • glue • button • needle and thread • yarn or cord • beads • glitter

1. Enlarge the pattern (left) and use it to cut out your pouch. Cut one shape following line A for the back and flap, and one following line B for the front.

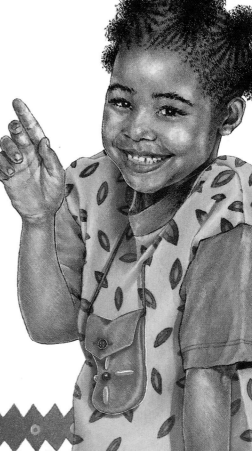

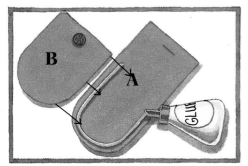

2. Sew the button onto piece B where the X is, as shown. Glue piece B over piece A with the button on the outside. Let the glue dry.

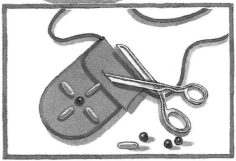

3. Fold the flap over. Carefully cut a hole for the button in the flap. Decorate with pieces of fabric, beads, or glitter. Wear with pride!

The Nguzo Saba (EN-goo-zoh-SAH-bah)

That's Swahili for "seven principles." The seven principles are a very important part of Kwanzaa. Each principle is a value or a goal that we should practice and live by all year long. There is one principle for each day of Kwanzaa.

Day 1

UMOJA ★ Unity

The first day of Kwanzaa emphasizes the need to work for and keep unity in your family, among your friends, and in your neighborhood. We strive for peace everywhere by living in harmony, and playing and working together.

Unity Dolls

You will need
brown construction paper • yarn • fabric scraps • scissors

1. Fold the construction paper in half and then in half again. Draw and cut out a doll figure. Be careful not to cut across the hands.

2. Open it up and you will have four dolls connected at the hands. Paste yarn and scrap pieces of fabric to each doll for hair and clothes.

Unity dolls need to hold hands in order to stand up. Use tape to connect the dolls on each end at the hands.

Afrocentric Vest

You will need
large brown paper bag • scissors • fabric scraps or markers

1. Open up the paper bag and mark it as shown. Cut along the lines, cutting out front and neck openings. Also make two cuts across the bottom sides of the bag.

2. Have an adult press the bag flat with an iron on low heat. Draw lines for the arm holes, as shown. Make sure they are big enough for you and then cut them out.

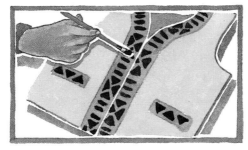

3. Decorate in traditional African patterns by gluing on scraps of fabric, or draw your designs with markers or crayons.

KUJICHAGULIA ★ Self Determination

The second day of Kwanzaa concentrates on deciding for yourself, believing in yourself, and taking responsibility for your own decisions and actions.

 **Jigsaw Puzzle**

You will need
old magazines • scissors • glue • empty cereal box

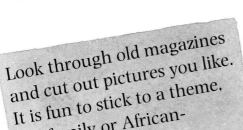

Look through old magazines and cut out pictures you like. It is fun to stick to a theme, like family or African-American history.

1. Cut out the front of the box to use as a base. Cut out your pictures from old magazines and place them overlapping each other on the cardboard.

3. Draw wiggly jigsaw lines on the back of the puzzle. Cut out the shapes. Have your friends put the puzzle back together. Can they guess the theme?

2. Once you have covered all the space on the cardboard and have the pictures the way you want, paste them in position. Make sure each picture is glued down completely. Let dry.

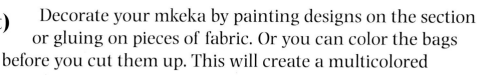

Mkeka (African Mat)

You will need
2-3 grocery bags
• tape • fabric scraps
• paint or coloring pens
• ruler • scissors • pencil

Decorate your mkeka by painting designs on the section or gluing on pieces of fabric. Or you can color the bags before you cut them up. This will create a multicolored design when you weave.

1. Pull apart the seam in the back and at the bottom of the bag. Flatten the bag and cut it the long way into strips three inches wide.

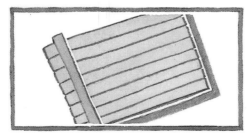

2. Lay 8 strips together on a flat surface, set the remaining strips aside. Use tape to hold down one side of the strips, leaving at least 2 inches at the ends. Now you are ready to weave.

3. Take one of the remaining strips and go over and under the flat strips. The next strip should go under and over in the opposite sequence. The strip after that should go over and under again.

4. Leave about 2 inches unwoven on the bottom and around the sides. Then fold all the ends under and tape them securely, carefully working your way around each edge of your mkeka.

UJIMA ★ Collective Work and Responsibility

The third day of Kwanzaa focuses on working together. We work together to help others and to build a better community. We also work together to find solutions to problems and to overcome hardship.

🔵 African Mask

You will need
a balloon • newspapers • 2 cups flour • 4 cups warm water • ½ cup white glue • paints (various colors) • scissors

1. Mix the flour, water, and glue into a paste. Tear up old newspapers into strips. Dip the strips into the paste.

2. Cover the balloon with a layer of strips. Let dry thoroughly. Pop the balloon. Cut in half the long way.

3. Attach cardboard ears with tape. Cut out eyes. Cover the entire mask with several layers of newspaper.

4. When the mask is dry, paint it. You can also decorate your mask with things like beads or yarn.

Traditionally, Africans wore masks to feel brave in battle and when hunting. Today, masks are also worn for celebrations such as birth, marriage, or harvest.

Nguzo Saba Mobile

You will need
paper plate • cardboard • hole punch • stapler • paint • yarn • scissors

1. Draw a spiral on the paper plate as shown. Carefully cut along this line. Cut out seven squares of cardboard (one for each principle) to hang from the mobile.

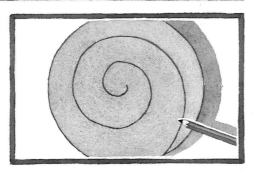

2. Pierce a hole at the top of each square with the hole punch. Pierce holes through the paper plate, with one through the middle. Tie a piece of yarn to each square and thread the other end through a hole in the plate. Secure with a large knot.

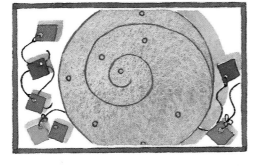

3. Decorate the squares and the paper plate with the seven principles. Tie one more piece of yarn through the hole in the middle of the paper plate. Your mobile is ready to hang!

You can make many other types of mobile too. Try a safari mobile with African animals, or a family mobile with pictures of the members of your family, or a friend mobile.

UJAMAA ★ Cooperative Economics

The fourth day of Kwanzaa is about using our money and talents wisely so that we all may prosper. We cooperate by sharing money, taking responsibility for our work, buying things together, and using our money to help others who are in need.

Savings Bank

You will need
4 toilet-paper tubes • colored paper • plastic wrap • tape scissors • glue • small block of wood

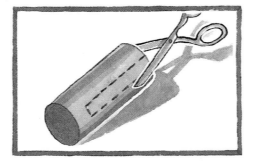

1. This bank will hold pennies, nickels, dimes, and quarters. Use scissors to cut a strip out of each of the four tubes, as shown.

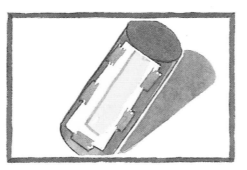

2. Cover each hole with a piece of plastic wrap. Tape it in place. This will be the window through which you can watch your savings grow.

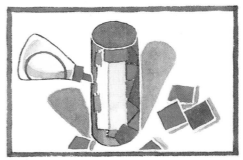

3. Decorate the outside of each tube with a mosaic of paper. Let dry. Glue the tubes onto a wooden block or piece of heavy cardboard.

African Trade Beads

African trade beads are beautiful multicolored beads that were used to trade with African merchants in the 1800s. You can make your own.

For more complicated beads, roll some clay flat between two sheets of wax paper with a rolling pin to make a sheet of clay. Remove wax paper and cut out shapes with a butter knife. Stick them together to make just about anything!

Rub cold clay between your hands to soften. Square or round beads made from one color of clay are the easiest to make.

To make multicolored beads, roll different colors of long round logs together. Place several logs together and slice to reveal a pattern. Take tiny bits of different colors and stick them together to form swirly beads.

Use toothpicks to make holes in the beads. Follow the instructions on the package for baking. String beads together to make necklaces or bracelets. To connect, attach clasps or tie a large bead to one end and make a loop in the other.

19

Nia ★ Purpose

The fifth day of Kwanzaa reminds us to have a plan for the future and to use our talents and abilities to achieve that purpose. When we can, we should also help others to develop their talents and achieve their goals.

Book Holder

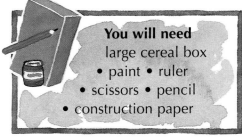

You will need
large cereal box
• paint • ruler
• scissors • pencil
• construction paper

This holder can be used to store books that are related to your purpose or can help you achieve it.

1. Make sure your cereal box is large enough to hold your books or magazines. Carefully cut off the top part of the box as shown.

2. Decorate by covering with a collage of colored paper. You could also decorate with leftover wallpaper or your favorite stickers.

Nia Scroll

You will need
scrap of fabric • red or green construction paper • scissors • glue • 12 inches of ribbon • marker

Tie your scroll with ribbon and put it in a secret place. Read it next Kwanzaa— see if your purpose has changed.

NIA — Purpose
My purpose is to be positive.

1. You can make 4 scrolls with one piece of paper. Cut the construction paper into 4 strips the long way. Use one strip of paper as a pattern to cut out a strip of fabric.

Terrarium

You will need
large jar • pebbles • charcoal • potting
soil, small plants (ferns, ivy, moss)
• rocks • sticks

Put $^1/_2$ inch of pebbles in the bottom of
the jar, then put $^1/_2$ inch of charcoal on
top of the pebbles. Next put about 4
inches of potting soil on top of the
charcoal. Place the plants in an attractive
arrangement in the jar. Add a little water
to make the soil damp. Add a few sticks
and rocks to make it scenic. Screw on the
lid of the jar and have an
adult poke a few holes in
the lid. Add a few drops
of water each week.
Place the jar in a sunny
place and watch your
plants grow.

2. Spread glue on one side of the
paper. Glue the cloth to the paper
so it fits exactly. Let it dry. Write
the word "NIA" on the left side of
the paper and write your purpose
on the right side.

KUUMBA ★ Creativity

Day 6

The sixth day of Kwanzaa is about expressing yourself creatively through music, art, dance, and thought. Kuumba is also about beautifying your living environment, such as your home or neighborhood.

♦ Tambourine

You will need
2 aluminum pie pans • ribbons (red, green, and black) • hole punch • 4 small bells • stapler • scissors

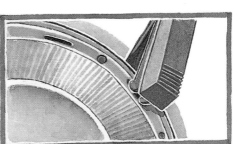

♦ Horn

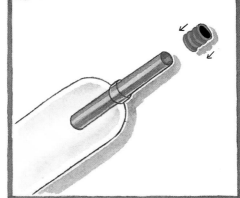

1. Ask an adult to cut off the bottom of a plastic bottle and to cut off the top part of a second plastic bottle to make a mouthpiece.

2. Roll some thin cardboard up to fit inside the plastic bottle. Take the "mouthpiece" and fit it on top of the tube. Secure everything with tape.

1. Place the brims of the two pie pans together and staple them in four places. Use the hole punch to make four holes in the brim of the pie pan.

2. Cut four pieces of ribbon 12 inches long. Thread each ribbon through a bell and tie it through one of the holes. Decorate by stapling extra ribbons around the brim.

Scrapper

Cut two pieces of sandpaper and glue them to two small blocks of wood. Rub together for an interesting sound.

African Rain Stick

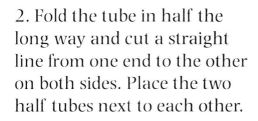

You will need
long cardboard tube (empty gift wrap roll) • piece of flat cardboard • scissors • masking tape • pen • 2½ cups of split peas • paint • yarn

1. Use the bottom of the tube to trace seven circles on the flat cardboard. Cut out the circles. Cut five circles in half, leaving the other two whole.

2. Fold the tube in half the long way and cut a straight line from one end to the other on both sides. Place the two half tubes next to each other.

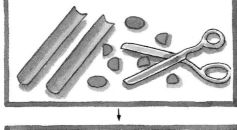

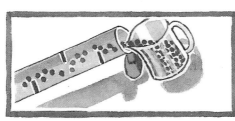

4. Pour the peas into the tube. Close with the last cardboard circle and tape. Wrap masking tape around the entire tube. Decorate. Turn the stick upside down and listen to the "rain."

3. Securely tape five half circles to the inside of each tube. Make sure that the half circles do not touch each other and tape the tube back together again. Tape one end closed with a cardboard circle.

Imani ★ Faith

The seventh day of Kwanzaa teaches us to believe with all our heart in our people, our parents, our teachers, and our leaders. We also believe in ourselves and our ability to succeed—as individuals and as a people.

Kwanzaa Memory Book

You will need
large sheet of construction paper • pencil • scissors • cardboard • glue • paints

1. Cut the construction paper into three strips the long way. This will be enough to make three books, so you could make Kwanzaa memory books to give as gifts for your family and friends.

2. Fold one strip in half. Then fold it in half twice more to make 8 panels. Cut two squares from the cardboard, each the size of one panel. Glue the squares to the outside panels.

3. Paint and decorate the cover of your book. Record the events of each day of Kwanzaa as they happen.

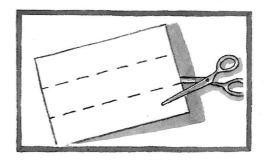

◉ Blindfold Adventure ◉ Treasure box

You will need
blindfolds for half of the players

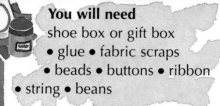

You will need
shoe box or gift box
● glue ● fabric scraps
● beads ● buttons ● ribbon
● string ● beans

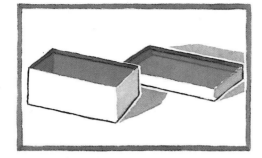

This is a good game to play at Kwanzaa or during family get-togethers.

1. Line the inside of the box with a large scrap of fabric, gluing it securely around the top edges. Use ribbon to line the inside borders.

2. Paint the outside and decorate it with ribbon, yarn, feathers, buttons. Keep your Kwanzaa treasures safely inside.

Divide the players into teams of two. The partner who goes first puts on the blindfold. The other partner is the protector. It is the protector's duty to take the blindfolded partner around the room or house and to protect them from any danger. See what happens when you trust and cooperate with your partner. See what happens when you don't. Get ready, get set, go! Reverse roles for the next adventure.

Kwanzaa Karamu

The Kwanzaa karamu is a lavish feast and cultural program that takes place on December 31. All are welcomed, and everyone brings a dish to share. The room is decorated in red, black, and green, and the seven Kwanzaa symbols are displayed prominently.

Program

Create a program for your Karamu celebration. Hand it out to your guests as they arrive.

KARAMU
* Welcome to all
* Introduction to newcomers
* Grandpa's story
* Slides and story of Aunt Djuana's trip to Africa
* Libation
* Feast

Napkin Rings

You will need
cardboard tubes • fabric scraps (red, green, black, or Afrocentric) • ruler • pencil • glue • scissors • beads • buttons • yarn

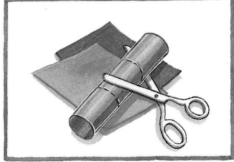

1. Measure 1 or 2 inches along the length of the cardboard tube. Cut out as many rings as you need.

2. Glue strips of fabric to the rings and decorate with yarn, beads, or paper. Add napkins and prepare to feast!

Coasters

You will need
thick red, black, and green yarn • plastic tops from butter or coffee containers • glue

1. Cover the inside bottom of a plastic top with white glue.

2. Start at the rim and wind yarn around until you have covered the entire bottom. Let dry.

Kwanzaa Invitations

Make invitations for your Karamu feast from colored paper and other easy-to-find materials. Cut out maps of Africa from construction paper, or make miniature African masks. Don't forget to include the time and place of your celebration.

KWANZAA PARTY

KWANZAA PARTY

KWANZAA

Food for Kwanzaa

The recipes here are all simple to prepare and delicious to eat. Many of the ingredients are traditional African foods that grow in the tropics. Some of them even feature the Kwanzaa colors of red, green, and black! The recipes here are also suitable for Karamu. *Always* ask an adult to help you when you wish to use the kitchen, and take special care when working with sharp or hot things.

Finger delights

You will need
toothpicks • 1 can of pineapple chunks • 1 can of maraschino cherries • 2 bananas • 2 oranges • 2 apples • peanut butter

1. Drain the canned fruit. Peel and section oranges. Peel bananas. Cut apple in fourths and remove the core. Slice all the fruit into bite-sized pieces. Spread peanut butter on one side of the apples and the bananas if you wish.

2. Put a piece of orange, apple, and banana on a toothpick. Put a cherry, a piece of pineapple, and banana on another toothpick. The attractive and delicious combinations are endless! Serve chilled.

Ginger Beer

You will need
$\frac{1}{2}$ pound of ginger root
• $\frac{1}{3}$ cup lemon juice
• 1 cup honey • knife
• strainer

1. Ask an adult to slice the ginger, leaving the skin on. Place in a saucepan with 2 cups of water. Let simmer over medium heat for 30 minutes. Add honey, lemon juice. Set aside to cool.

Candied Sweet Potatoes

You will need
2 pounds sweet potatoes • 4 cups sugar • 1 orange • 1 lemon
• 1 stick of butter • 1 teaspoon cinnamon • ½ teaspoon nutmeg

1. Ask an adult to peel and slice the sweet potatoes. Put in a saucepan of water and put the lid on.

2. Let them gently boil for 25 minutes. Pour off most of the water and add the sugar, orange, lemon, butter, cinnamon, and nutmeg.

3. Cook the mixture uncovered over low heat. Have an adult stir it frequently so it doesn't stick and burn. It is finished when the potatoes are candied.

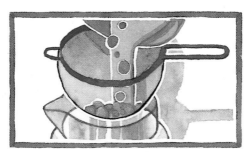

2. When the mixture is completely cool, pour it through the strainer into a large pitcher. Add another five cups of water and serve over ice.

Peanut Butter Stew

You will need

4 chicken quarters
2 teaspoons of flour
1½ cups milk
1½ cups chicken broth
1 cup peanut butter (creamy)
1 onion
1 green pepper
6 stalks celery
½ teaspoon salt
½ teaspoon pepper
cooking oil

Rice is a staple of most African and Caribbean dishes. It is also used in many traditional African-American dishes. This recipe requires rice as its base. You may use brown or white rice. Follow the directions for cooking on the rice box.

1. Put the chicken in a large pot with 6 cups of water. Bring to a boil, then simmer on low heat for ½ hour.

2. Add a little cooking oil to a frying pan. Sauté the onions, green peppers, and celery for 2-3 minutes.

4. Add the sautéed vegetables. Stir the liquid mixture into the pot. Cook on low heat, stirring often, for about an hour. Serve over rice.

3. Mix the flour, milk, chicken broth, peanut butter, salt, and pepper together in a bowl. Ask an adult to pour off half the liquid from the chicken pot.

Kwanzaa Salad

You will need
2 tomatoes • 1 red pepper
• 1 red onion • 1 can
black olives • lettuce •
spinach • oregano • large bowl

1. Wash all the vegetables and pat them dry with a clean dishcloth. Put equal amounts of spinach and lettuce in the bowl.

2. Ask an adult to help you chop the tomatoes, peppers, and onions. Add to bowl. Garnish with black olives and a dash of oregano.

3. Top with your favorite salad dressing. Now you have Kwanzaa colored salad!

Tropical Fruit Punch

You will need
1 1/2 cups pineapple juice
1/2 cup orange juice
1/2 cup lemon juice
1 1/4 cups cold water
1/2 teaspoon ground allspice
1 1/2 teaspoons grated lemon rind
2 tablespoons honey
3 cloves
1 liter ginger ale or lemon-lime soda
1 10-ounce package of frozen strawberries
punch bowl
ice tray

Set the frozen strawberries aside to thaw. Mix all the other ingredients in the punch bowl with the soda. When the strawberries have thawed, put one in each compartment of the ice tray. Fill the ice tray with some of the punch mixture and put it in the freezer. When the strawberry ice cubes have frozen, take them out of the ice tray and put them in glasses. Pour the remainder of the punch over them and serve—WOW! You can also use other fruit in the ice cubes, such as raspberries or cherries.

Corn Bread

You will need
2 cups self-rising buttermilk corn meal
1½ cups milk
1 egg
3 tablespoons vegetable oil
1-2 tablespoons sugar

1. Ask an adult to heat the oven to 425°F. In a large bowl mix the corn meal and sugar. Add the milk and egg and stir until blended. Add the oil and mix well.

2. Grease an 8-9 inch baking pan. Pour the mixture into the pan. Bake for 20-25 minutes, or until a wooden toothpick inserted in the center comes out clean.

Banana Pudding

You will need
1 box instant vanilla pudding • 1 box vanilla wafers • 2 cups milk • 2 bananas • large glass bowl

Follow directions on the box to make the vanilla pudding. Place a layer of vanilla wafers in the bottom of the large glass bowl. Add a layer of banana slices on top of the wafers. Then spread a layer of pudding on top of the bananas. Repeat this until you run out of ingredients. Garnish with a few banana slices on top. Delicious!